SECRETS TO BOOST YOUR CONFIDENCE

STRATEGIES FOR ACHIEVING YOUR DREAMS

DR. JAGADEESH PILLAI

Made with ♥ on the Notion Press Platform
www.notionpress.com

|| Dedicated to all wisdom seekers around the world ||

Contents

Contents

Prayer

"**Om Bhadram Karnebhih Shrunuyaama
DevaahBhadram Pashyemaakshabhiryajatraah
SthirairangaistushtuvaamsastanoobhihVyashema
Devahitam YadaayuhSwasti Na Indro
VridhashravaahSwasti Nah Pooshaa
VishwavedaahSwasti Nastaarkshyo ArishtanemihSwasti
No Brihaspatir DadhaatuOm Shantih, Shantih, Shantih**"

The literal meaning of this mantra is: OM. O Gods! Let us hear auspicious words from our ears. O reverent Gods! Let us behold propitious visions from our eyes, let our organs and body be stable, healthy, and strong. Let us do that which is pleasing to the gods in the life span allotted to us. May Indra, inscribed in the scriptures, bring us fortune! May Pushan, the knower of the world, grant us prosperity! May Trakshya, who vanquishes enemies, bestow us with blessings! May Brihaspati bring us success!
OM Peace, Peace, Peace.

❧❧❧

About The Author

Dr. Jagadeesh Pillai is a renowned Guinness World Record holder, writer, and researcher hailing from Varanasi, also known as the abode of Lord Shiva. With a Ph.D. in Vedic Science and a range of creative ideas and achievements, he is a true polymath. He is the author of more than 100 books including Research Publications. Although his roots can be traced back to Kerala, the people of Varanasi hold him in high regard and affectionately consider him one of their own.

In 1998, Dr. Pillai was offered a job at Banaras Hindu University, but he left the position after only two months to pursue greater goals in life. He believed that in order to study Indian scriptures and engage in other creative endeavours, he needed to retire from the daily grind of working solely for money at a young age.

He started an export business from scratch, using the knowledge he had gained from a previous job in the industry. His intelligence and unique approach to business led to great success in a short period of time, earning him more in just a decade and a half than he would have in a lifetime working in a government job. Upon the passing of Dr. APJ Abdul Kalam, Dr. Pillai decided to leave the business and dedicate himself to reading, studying, researching, and experimenting.

During his tenure in the export business, Dr. Pillai traveled to over 16 countries, gaining valuable insight and experiencing the world and life in detail.

Dr. Pillai has achieved four Guinness World Records in the following subjects:

"Script to Screen" - In this record, Dr. Pillai produced and directed an animation film within the shortest time possible, breaking the previous record set by Canadians. He has also received numerous national and international awards and recognitions for this achievement.

Longest Line of Postcards - For this record, Dr. Pillai created a line of 16,300 postcards on the occasion of the 163rd anniversary of Indian Postal Day. The event also included a questionnaire about the Indian flag.

Largest Poster Awareness Campaign - Dr. Pillai designed an awareness campaign on the subject of "Beti Bachao - Beti Padhao" (Save the Girl Child - Educate the Girl Child) to achieve this record.

Largest Envelope - In tribute to the Indian Prime Minister's "Make in India" initiative, Dr. Pillai created a 4000 square meter envelope using waste paper to achieve this record.

Attempted - **70000 Candles on a 210 kg Cake** - To celebrate the 70th Indian Independence Day, Dr. Pillai attempted to light 70,000 candles on a 210 kg cake, which was recorded in World Records India.

Attempted - **Documentary on Dhamek Stupa of Sarnath in 17 Languages** - Dr. Pillai attempted to create a documentary on the Dhamek Stupa of Sarnath, dubbing it in 17 different languages. The result of this attempt is currently awaiting confirmation from the Guinness World Records.

Dr. Pillai is skilled in teaching the Bhagavad Gita, a Hindu scripture, and is popular among young people. He has helped many young people improve their lives through his motivational teachings.

In addition to teaching, he has composed and sung numerous Sanskrit Bhajans and patriotic songs.

He has also written and directed several short films and documentaries for awareness campaigns, and has volunteered with the police in both UP and Kerala to spread awareness about various issues through videos and photography.

Incredibly, he has produced and directed over 100 documentaries about the city of Varanasi, all on his own.

He has also helped and guided more than 25 boys and girls to achieve world records through creative and innovative methods. He is a multifaceted person who uses his intellect and the blessings given to him by God to excel in various areas. He is both a teacher and a student, always learning and teaching, and is able to master any subject he comes across.

He is a selfless social activist and motivational speaker who has overcome struggles and failures to become a successful and enthusiastic individual with a rich life experience.

In addition to his work with the Bhagavad Gita, he is also an efficient Tarot card reader, Astro-Vastu consultant, and a talented singer and composer. He has sung the entire Ram Charita Manas and Bhagavad Gita in his own compositions, and has sung the phrase "Lokah Samastha Sukhino Bhavantu" in 50 different languages. He is currently working on a detailed and scientific study of Vedas, Upanishads, Puranas, and the Bhagavad Gita. He has also composed and sung the Hanuman Chalisa and Gayatri Mantra in 108 and 1008 different compositions, respectively.

Awards - Four Times Guinness World Records, Winner of Mahatma Gandhi Vishwa Shanti Puraskar, Mahatma Gandhi Global Peace Ambassador, Kashi Ratna Award, Dr. APJ Abdul Kalam Motivational Person of the Year 2017, Mother Teresa Award, Indira Gandhi Priyadarshini Award, Bharat Vikas Ratna Award, Udyog Ratna Award, Vigyan Prasar Award, Poorvanchal Ratn Samman.

ॐॐॐ

Preface

In this book, "Secrets to Boost Your Confidence Strategies for Achieving Your Dream," we will be exploring various techniques and strategies for developing self-confidence and achieving success in life. Confidence is a crucial component in reaching our goals and realizing our full potential. Without it, we may find ourselves feeling defeated and unmotivated, unable to move forward in pursuit of our dreams.

In this book, we will delve into different aspects of confidence building, from understanding our strengths and weaknesses, to setting and achieving goals, to managing stress and making healthy choices. We will also explore the importance of self-compassion, positive thinking, and living in the moment.

We will also discuss the role of support systems in building confidence, and the impact that negative thoughts and beliefs can have on our self-esteem. We will explore ways to reframe our perspectives, embrace change, and cultivate self-trust and self-esteem.

Ultimately, this book aims to provide a comprehensive guide to building self-confidence and achieving success in life. By following the strategies outlined in this book, you can learn to overcome fears and obstacles, and take control of your life, unlocking your full potential and living your best life.

❦❦❦

ONE

Developing an Attitude of Confidence

Confidence is a crucial factor in determining our success and happiness in life. Having confidence means believing in yourself and your abilities, and it allows you to take risks and face challenges with courage and determination. However, building confidence can be a challenge, especially if you have a history of negative self-talk or past experiences that have shaken your confidence. But with the right tools and strategies, you can develop an attitude of confidence that will help you achieve your dreams and live a fulfilling life.

Practice self-affirmation Self-affirmations are positive statements that you repeat to yourself regularly. These statements help to counteract negative self-talk and reinforce positive thoughts and beliefs about yourself. Examples of self-affirmations include, "I am worthy and capable of achieving my goals" or "I am confident in my abilities." Repeat these affirmations to yourself every day, especially when you're feeling down or uncertain.

Surround yourself with positive people The people you spend time with can have a significant impact on your attitude and confidence. Surrounding yourself with positive, supportive individuals who believe in you and your abilities can help boost your confidence and make you feel good about yourself.

Take care of yourself Taking care of your physical and emotional well-being is crucial to building confidence. This includes getting enough sleep, eating well, exercising regularly, and engaging in activities that bring you joy and relaxation. When you feel good physically and emotionally, it shows in your confidence and self-assurance.

Set achievable goals Setting and achieving goals is a great way to boost confidence. Start by setting small, achievable goals that you can complete within a short period. As you complete each goal, you will feel a sense of accomplishment and it will motivate you to set and achieve even bigger goals.

Face your fears Fear can be a major barrier to confidence. Facing your fears head-on can help you overcome them and build your confidence. Start by identifying the things that you're afraid of and make a plan to face them. Whether it's public speaking or trying a new activity, taking small steps towards facing your fears can help you overcome them and build your confidence.

Celebrate your successes Celebrating your successes, no

matter how small, is important for building confidence. Acknowledge your achievements and give yourself credit for all that you've accomplished. This will help you recognize your strengths and abilities, which will in turn boost your confidence.

In conclusion, developing an attitude of confidence takes time and effort, but it is achievable with the right strategies and tools. By practicing self-affirmations, surrounding yourself with positive people, taking care of yourself, setting achievable goals, facing your fears, and celebrating your successes, you can build a strong foundation of confidence that will serve you throughout your life.

ᛒᛒᛒ

"Confidence is not 'they will like me.'
Confidence is 'I'll be fine if they don't.'"

TWO
NEGATIVE THOUGHTS AND BELIEFS

Negative thoughts and beliefs can have a profound impact on our confidence and self-esteem. When we repeatedly tell ourselves that we are not good enough, not smart enough, or not capable enough, it can lead to a cycle of low confidence and self-doubt. In this chapter, we will explore the impact of negative thoughts and beliefs on our confidence and provide strategies for overcoming them.

Recognize and challenge negative thoughts The first step in overcoming negative thoughts and beliefs is to recognize when they are happening. Pay attention to your self-talk and notice when you are engaging in negative thinking. Once you recognize these negative thoughts, challenge them. Ask yourself if they are really true and what evidence you have to support them. Replace negative thoughts with more positive, supportive thoughts.

Practice gratitude Focusing on what we are grateful for can help shift our focus away from negative thoughts and beliefs. Make a habit of writing down three things you are grateful for each day. This will help you see the good in your life and shift your focus away from negative thoughts and beliefs.

Surround yourself with positive people Surrounding yourself with positive, supportive individuals who believe in you and your abilities can help counteract negative thoughts and beliefs. Seek out relationships with people who are uplifting and who encourage you to be your best self.

Engage in self-care Self-care is crucial in overcoming negative thoughts and beliefs. When we take care of ourselves physically and emotionally, we are better equipped to deal with negative thoughts and beliefs. Engage in activities that bring you joy and relaxation, and make time for self-reflection and introspection.

Embrace failure Failure is a natural part of the learning and growth process. When we embrace failure and view it as a learning opportunity, we can shift our focus away from negative thoughts and beliefs and start to see our failures as stepping stones to success.

Seek support Finally, seeking support from a trusted friend, family member, or mental health professional can be invaluable in overcoming negative thoughts and beliefs. Talking to someone about your feelings and concerns can help you gain a new perspective and feel more confident in your abilities.

In conclusion, negative thoughts and beliefs can have a significant impact on our confidence and self-esteem. By recognizing and challenging negative thoughts, practicing gratitude, surrounding ourselves with positive people, engaging in self-care, embracing failure, and seeking support, we can overcome negative thoughts and beliefs and build a foundation of confidence that will serve us throughout our lives.

ᙏᙏᙏ

"Believe in yourself and all that you are.
Know that there is something inside you that
is greater than any obstacle."

♡♡♡

THREE

UNDERSTANDING YOUR STRENGTHS AND WEAKNESSES

In order to build confidence and achieve our goals, it's important to understand our strengths and weaknesses. By identifying what we excel at and what areas we need to improve upon, we can make a plan to develop our skills and maximize our potential. In this chapter, we will explore how to understand your strengths and weaknesses, and how to use this information to build your confidence.

Assess your skills and abilities One way to understand your strengths and weaknesses is to assess your skills and abilities. You can do this through self-reflection or by taking personality or skills assessments. Ask yourself what you enjoy doing, what you excel at, and what you find challenging. This information can help you identify your areas of strength and weakness.

Seek feedback from others Another way to understand your strengths and weaknesses is to seek feedback from others. Ask friends, family, co-workers, or even a mentor for their honest opinions on your strengths and weaknesses. Be open to constructive criticism, and use the feedback to identify areas you need to work on.

Keep a skills log Keeping a skills log can be an effective way to understand your strengths and weaknesses. Keep track of what you have learned and what skills you have developed. This can help you see your progress and identify areas you need to improve upon.

Embrace challenges Embracing challenges can help you understand your strengths and weaknesses. Try new things, step outside your comfort zone, and see what you are capable of. This can help you build new skills and identify areas that need improvement.

Focus on your strengths Once you have a good understanding of your strengths and weaknesses, focus on your strengths. Play to your strengths and develop your skills in these areas. This will help you feel more confident and capable.

Work on your weaknesses While it's important to focus on your strengths, it's also important to work on your weaknesses. Identify areas that need improvement and make a plan to develop your skills. Seek training or coaching if necessary, and be patient with yourself as you work on improving.

In conclusion, understanding your strengths and weaknesses is an important step in building confidence and achieving your goals. By assessing your skills and abilities, seeking feedback from others, keeping a skills log, embracing challenges, focusing on your strengths, and working on your weaknesses, you can develop a better understanding of yourself and build your confidence. By embracing your strengths and working on your weaknesses, you can become the best version of yourself and achieve your dreams.

ppp

"Confidence is not the absence of fear, but the
triumph over it."

❦❦❦

FOUR

SETTING AND ACHIEVING GOALS

Setting and achieving goals is an important step in building confidence and realizing your dreams. When you have clear, achievable goals, you have a roadmap to follow and can measure your progress along the way. In this chapter, we will explore how to set and achieve goals in a way that will boost your confidence and help you achieve success.

Identify your goals The first step in setting and achieving goals is to identify what you want to achieve. Consider your long-term and short-term goals, as well as personal, professional, and financial goals. Write your goals down and be specific about what you want to achieve.

Make a plan Once you have identified your goals, make a plan to achieve them. Break down your goals into smaller, achievable steps, and create a timeline for completing each step. Consider what resources you will need and what obstacles you may encounter.

Prioritize your goals Prioritize your goals based on their importance to you. Focus on the goals that are most important and will have the greatest impact on your life. This will help you stay focused and motivated.

Stay accountable Stay accountable to your goals by tracking your progress and holding yourself accountable for achieving them. Consider working with a coach or accountability partner to help you stay on track.

Celebrate your successes As you achieve your goals, take the time to celebrate your successes. Celebrating your successes will help you build confidence and stay motivated to continue pursuing your goals.

Learn from your failures When you experience setbacks or fail to achieve a goal, don't give up. Instead, use these experiences as opportunities to learn and grow. Consider what you can do differently next time and adjust your plan accordingly.

In conclusion, setting and achieving goals is a key component of building confidence and realizing your dreams. By identifying your goals, making a plan, prioritizing your goals, staying accountable, celebrating your successes, and learning from your failures, you can achieve your goals and boost your confidence along the way. Remember to be patient, persistent, and stay focused on your goals. With hard work and determination, you can achieve anything you set your mind to.

DR. JAGADEESH PILLAI

❦❦❦

"The greatest barrier to success is the fear of failure."

♥♥♥

FIVE

TURNING FEAR INTO ACTION

Fear can be a major obstacle to confidence and success. It can hold us back from taking risks, trying new things, and pursuing our dreams. However, with the right strategies and techniques, it is possible to turn fear into action and boost your confidence in the process. In this chapter, we will explore how to turn fear into action and take control of your life.

Identify your fears The first step in turning fear into action is to identify what you are afraid of. Consider what is holding you back and what specific fears are preventing you from taking action. Write your fears down and be specific about what you are afraid of.

Challenge your fears Once you have identified your fears, challenge them. Ask yourself if your fears are rational or irrational. If your fears are irrational, try to reframe your thinking and focus on the positive outcomes of taking action.

Take small steps Start small and take gradual steps towards facing your fears. This will help you build confidence and reduce anxiety.

Focus on your strengths Focus on your strengths and what you are good at. This will help you build confidence and feel more in control.

Seek support Seek support from friends, family, or a therapist. Talking to someone about your fears can help you feel less alone and provide you with valuable insights and strategies for overcoming your fears.

Reward yourself As you face your fears and take action, reward yourself for your efforts. Celebrating your successes will help you build confidence and stay motivated to continue facing your fears.

Learn from your experiences When you experience setbacks or fail to overcome a fear, don't give up. Instead, use these experiences as opportunities to learn and grow. Consider what you can do differently next time and adjust your approach accordingly.

In conclusion, turning fear into action is a key component of building confidence and achieving your dreams. By identifying your fears, challenging your fears, taking small steps, focusing on your strengths, seeking support, rewarding yourself, and learning from your experiences, you can overcome your fears and boost your confidence along the way. Remember to be patient, persistent, and stay focused on your goals. With hard work and determination, you can achieve anything you set your mind to.

♡♡♡

"Confidence comes not from always being right but from not fearing to be wrong."

♥♥♥

SIX

TAKING RISKS AND PUSHING YOUR LIMITS

Self-compassion and self-care are essential components of building confidence and achieving your dreams. When you prioritize self-compassion and self-care, you create a supportive and nurturing environment for yourself, which allows you to build confidence and resilience in the face of challenges and setbacks. In this chapter, we will explore the benefits of self-compassion and self-care and provide tips for incorporating these practices into your life.

Understanding self-compassion Self-compassion involves treating yourself with the same kindness, care, and understanding that you would offer to a good friend. It means acknowledging your feelings, accepting your limitations, and recognizing that everyone makes mistakes.

Benefits of self-compassion Self-compassion has been

linked to a number of positive outcomes, including increased well-being, reduced anxiety and depression, and improved resilience. It can also help you build confidence and feel more capable of pursuing your goals.

Incorporating self-compassion into your life To practice self-compassion, try to adopt a kind and understanding attitude towards yourself. Avoid self-criticism and instead focus on self-forgiveness. Surround yourself with positive and supportive people, and engage in activities that bring you joy and fulfillment.

Understanding self-care Self-care involves taking care of your physical, emotional, and mental well-being. It includes activities like exercise, sleep, eating well, and engaging in hobbies and interests.

Benefits of self-care Self-care has been linked to improved health and well-being, reduced stress and anxiety, and increased energy and focus. When you prioritize self-care, you also build resilience and become better equipped to handle the challenges and setbacks that come with pursuing your goals.

Incorporating self-care into your life To prioritize self-care, make a habit of engaging in activities that support your physical, emotional, and mental well-being. Find ways to fit self-care into your daily routine, and be mindful of your needs and boundaries.

In conclusion, practicing self-compassion and self-care are important components of building confidence and achieving your dreams. By embracing self-compassion and self-care, you can create a supportive and nurturing environment for yourself, build resilience, and become better equipped to handle the challenges and setbacks that come with pursuing your goals. So prioritize self-compassion and self-care, and watch as your confidence and success grow in the process.

ppp

"You are never too old to set another goal or
to dream a new dream."

ᗐᗐᗐ

SEVEN

PRACTICING SELF-COMPASSION AND SELF-CARE

Connecting with others and building supportive relationships can play a critical role in building confidence and achieving your dreams. When you have a supportive network of people in your life, you have access to encouragement, advice, and help when you need it. In this chapter, we will explore the importance of connecting with others and finding support, and provide tips for building and maintaining positive relationships.

Understanding the importance of social support Social support is essential for building confidence, reducing stress, and achieving your goals. When you have a supportive network of people in your life, you feel more connected and confident, and are better equipped to handle challenges and setbacks.

Building relationships Building relationships involves making connections with others and actively working to maintain those connections. To build positive relationships, try to be open and friendly, listen actively, and be there for others when they need support.

Finding support in your community Your community can be a great source of support, and there are many opportunities to connect with others and build relationships. Try to get involved in local organizations and activities that interest you, and look for opportunities to volunteer and help others.

Leveraging technology Technology can also provide opportunities to connect with others and build relationships. Consider using social media to connect with friends and family, or participate in online forums and communities to connect with people who share your interests.

Maintaining positive relationships To maintain positive relationships, be proactive about keeping in touch with friends and family, and make an effort to listen and support others when they need it. Be honest and open about your own needs and boundaries, and try to avoid engaging in negative or destructive behavior.

In conclusion, connecting with others and finding support is an important part of building confidence and achieving your dreams. By building and maintaining positive relationships, you have access to encouragement, advice, and help when you need it, which can help you feel more connected, confident, and capable of pursuing your goals.

So prioritize connecting with others and finding support, and watch as your confidence and success grow in the process.

❦❦❦

"Success is not final, failure is not fatal: it is
the courage to continue that counts."

ϷϷϷ

EIGHT

CONNECTING WITH PEOPLE AND FINDING SUPPORT

In order to build confidence and achieve your dreams, it is important to take care of yourself and manage stress in healthy ways. In this chapter, we will discuss the importance of making healthy choices and managing stress, and provide tips for creating a healthy lifestyle and reducing stress in your life.

Understanding the impact of lifestyle on confidence and stress The choices you make in terms of diet, exercise, and other habits can have a significant impact on your confidence and stress levels. When you make healthy choices, you feel better physically and mentally, which can help boost your confidence and reduce stress.

Eating for confidence and well-being Eating a balanced, nutritious diet can help you feel better physically and mentally, and can also help reduce stress and boost your confidence. Try to eat a variety of healthy foods, and avoid processed or junk foods that can leave you feeling sluggish and stressed.

Exercise and physical activity Exercise and physical activity are important for both physical and mental health. Regular physical activity can help reduce stress, boost your confidence, and improve your overall well-being. Consider incorporating a mix of cardio, strength training, and mindfulness practices into your routine.

Getting enough sleep Getting enough sleep is essential for good physical and mental health, and can help you feel more energized, confident, and able to handle stress. Make a habit of going to bed and waking up at the same time each day, and try to limit exposure to screens before bedtime.

Managing stress Stress can be overwhelming and can impact your confidence and well-being. To manage stress, try to identify the sources of stress in your life, and develop strategies for reducing or eliminating them. Consider incorporating relaxation and mindfulness practices into your routine, and take time for self-care and hobbies that you enjoy.

In conclusion, making healthy choices and managing stress are important for building confidence and achieving your dreams. By taking care of yourself and reducing stress in healthy ways, you can improve your overall well-being, feel more confident, and be better equipped to handle challenges and setbacks as you pursue your goals. So prioritize making healthy choices and managing stress, and watch as your confidence and success grow in the process.

❦❦❦

"Confidence is the foundation of all great successes."

♡♡♡

NINE

Making Healthy Choices and Managing Stress

In order to build confidence and achieve your dreams, it is important to take care of yourself and manage stress in healthy ways. In this chapter, we will discuss the importance of making healthy choices and managing stress, and provide tips for creating a healthy lifestyle and reducing stress in your life

Understanding the impact of lifestyle on confidence and stress The choices you make in terms of diet, exercise, and other habits can have a significant impact on your confidence and stress levels. When you make healthy choices, you feel better physically and mentally, which can help boost your confidence and reduce stress.

Eating for confidence and well-being Eating a balanced, nutritious diet can help you feel better physically and mentally, and can also help reduce stress and boost your confidence. Try to eat a variety of healthy foods, and avoid processed or junk foods that can leave you feeling sluggish and stressed.

Exercise and physical activity Exercise and physical activity are important for both physical and mental health. Regular physical activity can help reduce stress, boost your confidence, and improve your overall well-being. Consider incorporating a mix of cardio, strength training, and mindfulness practices into your routine.

Getting enough sleep Getting enough sleep is essential for good physical and mental health, and can help you feel more energized, confident, and able to handle stress. Make a habit of going to bed and waking up at the same time each day, and try to limit exposure to screens before bedtime.

Managing stress Stress can be overwhelming and can impact your confidence and well-being. To manage stress, try to identify the sources of stress in your life, and develop strategies for reducing or eliminating them. Consider incorporating relaxation and mindfulness practices into your routine, and take time for self-care and hobbies that you enjoy.

In conclusion, making healthy choices and managing stress are important for building confidence and achieving your dreams. By taking care of yourself and reducing stress in healthy ways, you can improve your overall well-being, feel more confident, and be better equipped to handle challenges and setbacks as you pursue your goals. So prioritize making healthy choices and managing stress, and watch as your confidence and success grow in the process.

❦❦❦

"Self-confidence is the first requisite to great undertakings."

♡♡♡

TEN

EMBRACING CHANGE AND TAKING CONTROL

Change can be scary and challenging, but it is also an opportunity to grow and develop. In this chapter, we will discuss the importance of embracing change and taking control of your life, and provide tips for navigating change and building confidence along the way.

Understanding change and its benefits Change is a natural part of life, and can bring new opportunities, growth, and development. By embracing change and being open to new experiences, you can expand your horizons, build your confidence, and achieve your dreams.

Overcoming fear of change Change can be scary, but it is also an opportunity to grow and develop. To overcome your fear of change, focus on the benefits and opportunities that change can bring, and take small steps towards embracing change and facing your fears.

Taking control of your life To build confidence and achieve your dreams, it is important to take control of your life and make choices that align with your goals and values. This means being proactive, setting boundaries, and making decisions that support your well-being and growth.

Embracing challenges as opportunities Challenges and setbacks are a natural part of the change and growth process, but they can also be opportunities to build your confidence and resilience. When faced with challenges, try to reframe them as opportunities for growth, and focus on the skills and strengths you can develop as you work through them.

Celebrating your successes and learning from failures Successes and failures are both important parts of the change and growth process, and they can help you build confidence and resilience as you work towards your goals. Celebrate your successes, learn from your failures, and use both to inform your journey and grow as a person.

In conclusion, embracing change and taking control of your life is essential for building confidence and achieving your dreams. By being open to new experiences, taking control of your life, embracing challenges, and celebrating your successes and failures, you can build your confidence, develop resilience, and achieve your goals. So embrace change and take control of your life, and watch as your confidence and success grow in the process.

ϷϷϷ

"Confidence is contagious. So is lack of confidence."

❥❥❥

ELEVEN

REFRAMING YOUR PERSPECTIVE AND THINKING POSITIVELY

Your thoughts and perspective have a powerful impact on your confidence and overall well-being. In this chapter, we will discuss the importance of reframing your perspective and thinking positively, and provide tips for shifting your thoughts and building a positive mindset.

Understanding the power of thoughts and perspective Your thoughts and perspective shape your beliefs and attitudes, and can have a significant impact on your confidence and overall well-being. By reframing your perspective and focusing on the positive, you can build your confidence and achieve your goals.

Identifying negative thought patterns Negative thought

patterns, such as self-doubt, criticism, and worry, can hold you back and undermine your confidence. To overcome these patterns, it is important to become aware of them and take steps to shift your thinking.

Reframing negative thoughts Reframing negative thoughts involves replacing them with positive, supportive thoughts that align with your goals and values. This can be done by focusing on the present moment, your strengths and successes, and your goals and aspirations.

Building a positive mindset Building a positive mindset involves adopting a positive outlook, focusing on the good in life, and cultivating gratitude. This can be achieved through practices such as mindfulness, journaling, and visualization, and can help build confidence and resilience.

Surrounding yourself with positive influences Surrounding yourself with positive influences, such as supportive friends and family, can also help you maintain a positive outlook and build your confidence. Seek out individuals who uplift and support you, and limit your exposure to negative influences that bring you down.

In conclusion, reframing your perspective and thinking positively is a key aspect of building confidence and achieving your goals. By shifting your thoughts, focusing on the positive, and surrounding yourself with supportive influences, you can build a positive mindset, increase your resilience, and achieve your dreams. So make the shift today, and watch as your confidence and success grow as a result.

ᔕᔕᔕ

"The only way to do great work is to love
what you do."

ᗷᗷᗷ

TWELVE

EXPRESSING YOURSELF AND CELEBRATING WHO YOU ARE

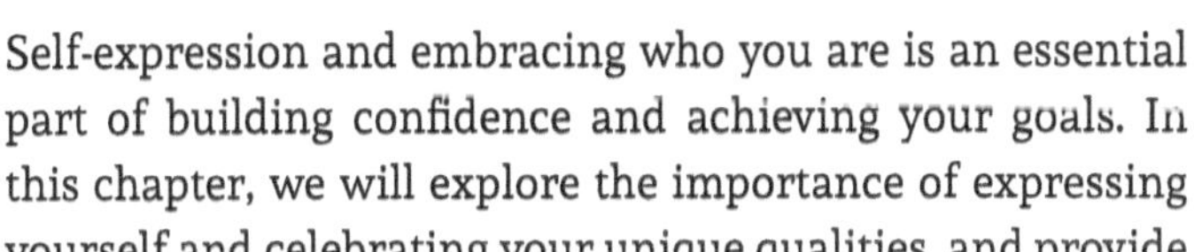

Self-expression and embracing who you are is an essential part of building confidence and achieving your goals. In this chapter, we will explore the importance of expressing yourself and celebrating your unique qualities, and provide tips for doing so effectively.

Understanding the importance of self-expression Self-expression is a powerful tool for building confidence and increasing your self-awareness. By expressing your thoughts, feelings, and desires, you can connect with others, gain a deeper understanding of who you are, and build self-confidence.

Embracing your uniqueness Embracing your uniqueness

means accepting and celebrating your individual strengths, weaknesses, and quirks. This can help build confidence by giving you a sense of purpose and direction, and by allowing you to stand out from the crowd.

Expressing yourself through creativity Expressing yourself through creativity, such as writing, drawing, painting, or playing music, can be a powerful form of self-expression. This can help you connect with others, build your confidence, and increase your self-awareness.

Finding your voice Finding your voice involves speaking up and sharing your opinions and thoughts with others. This can be challenging, but is essential for building confidence and developing meaningful relationships.

Celebrating your successes Celebrating your successes is an important part of embracing who you are and building confidence. Take time to acknowledge your accomplishments, no matter how big or small, and use this as motivation to keep moving forward.

In conclusion, expressing yourself and celebrating who you are is essential for building confidence and achieving your goals. By embracing your uniqueness, expressing yourself through creativity, finding your voice, and celebrating your successes, you can increase your self-awareness, build strong relationships, and achieve your dreams. So take the time to celebrate who you are, and let your confidence soar as a result.

ppp

"Confidence is a habit that can be developed
by acting as if you already have it."

ᐅᐅᐅ

THIRTEEN

CULTIVATING SELF-TRUST AND SELF-ESTEEM

Self-trust and self-esteem are crucial components of confidence and play a significant role in determining our ability to achieve our goals. In this chapter, we will explore the importance of self-trust and self-esteem, and provide tips for cultivating these qualities in yourself.

Understanding self-trust Self-trust refers to the belief in your own abilities, judgment, and decision-making. It is the foundation upon which confidence is built, and is essential for achieving your goals and living a fulfilling life.

Building self-trust Building self-trust involves acknowledging and accepting your limitations, setting achievable goals, and taking steps to achieve them. This can include seeking out new experiences, seeking feedback from others, and focusing on your strengths.

Understanding self-esteem Self-esteem refers to the overall value and worth you place on yourself. It is closely related to self-trust, and can impact your confidence and ability to achieve your goals.

Building self-esteem Building self-esteem involves focusing on your strengths and accomplishments, and letting go of negative self-talk and self-criticism. This can also include seeking out positive reinforcement from others, and surrounding yourself with supportive individuals.

Embracing self-care Self-care is an important aspect of cultivating self-trust and self-esteem. This includes taking care of your physical, emotional, and mental well-being, and making time for activities that bring you joy and fulfillment.

In conclusion, cultivating self-trust and self-esteem is essential for building confidence and achieving your goals. By focusing on your strengths, embracing self-care, and letting go of negative self-talk and self-criticism, you can increase your self-esteem and build a foundation of self-trust that will help you achieve your dreams. So take the time to cultivate self-trust and self-esteem, and watch your confidence soar as a result.

ᚦᚦᚦ

"The key to success is not just hard work, but smart work."

🖤🖤🖤

FOURTEEN

FOCUSING ON THE PRESENT AND LIVING IN THE MOMENT

One of the biggest obstacles to confidence is the tendency to get caught up in the past or worry about the future. By focusing on the present moment, we can cultivate a sense of peace, calm, and confidence that will serve as the foundation for achieving our goals.

The power of mindfulness Mindfulness is the practice of being present and fully engaged in the current moment, without judgment or distraction. By focusing on the present, we can reduce anxiety and stress, increase self-awareness, and cultivate a sense of inner peace.

The benefits of living in the moment Living in the moment has a number of benefits for our confidence and well-being.

By focusing on the present, we can reduce stress and anxiety, improve our relationships, and cultivate a sense of purpose and meaning.

Techniques for living in the moment There are a number of techniques that can help you cultivate a focus on the present moment. These can include meditation, mindfulness exercises, journaling, and spending time in nature.

Overcoming distractions and stressors Despite our best efforts, it can be difficult to stay focused on the present moment, especially when faced with distractions and stressors. However, by using mindfulness and stress-management techniques, we can learn to stay calm and focused in the face of these challenges.

Celebrating the present moment It's important to celebrate the present moment and acknowledge the good things that are happening in our lives. This can help us cultivate gratitude, a sense of inner peace, and a greater appreciation for the journey towards achieving our goals.

In conclusion, focusing on the present moment is a crucial component of building confidence and achieving our goals. By embracing mindfulness, living in the moment, and celebrating the present, we can cultivate a sense of peace, calm, and confidence that will help us achieve our dreams. So take the time to focus on the present, and watch as your confidence and well-being soar as a result.

ϸϸϸ

"The only limit to your impact is your self-esteem."

🖤🖤🖤

FIFTEEN

Achieving Balance and Embracing Happiness

Balancing the various demands of life can be a challenge, but finding balance and happiness is crucial for building confidence and achieving our goals. By prioritizing our well-being and embracing happiness, we can cultivate a positive outlook, reduce stress and anxiety, and become more motivated and focused on achieving our dreams.

The importance of balance Balancing the various demands of life can be challenging, but it is essential for our well-being and confidence. By finding balance in our relationships, work, and personal life, we can reduce stress, increase our sense of purpose, and improve our overall mood and outlook.

The benefits of happiness Embracing happiness has a number of benefits for our confidence and well-being. By prioritizing happiness and well-being, we can improve our relationships, reduce stress and anxiety, and cultivate a positive outlook and motivation to achieve our goals.

Techniques for finding balance and happiness There are a number of techniques that can help you achieve balance and happiness. These can include setting achievable goals, prioritizing self-care and self-compassion, practicing gratitude, and spending time with loved ones.

Overcoming obstacles to balance and happiness Despite our best efforts, it can be difficult to achieve balance and happiness, especially when faced with obstacles such as stress, relationship difficulties, and negative thinking patterns. However, by using mindfulness and stress-management techniques, we can learn to stay calm and focused in the face of these challenges and cultivate a positive outlook.

Celebrating balance and happiness It's important to celebrate the balance and happiness that we achieve, and acknowledge the good things in our lives. This can help us cultivate gratitude, a sense of inner peace, and a greater appreciation for the journey towards achieving our goals.

In conclusion, achieving balance and embracing happiness is a crucial component of building confidence and achieving our goals. By prioritizing our well-being and cultivating a positive outlook, we can reduce stress and anxiety, improve our relationships, and become more motivated and focused on achieving our dreams. So take the time to focus on your happiness and well-being, and watch as your confidence and sense of purpose soar as a result.

ഉഉഉ

"A lack of confidence holds us back from reaching our full potential, but with effort and dedication, we can overcome it and achieve greatness."

♥♥♥

Other Books Of The Author

1. The Moments When I Met God
2. Kashiyile Theertha Pathangal
3. GURU GYAN VANI
4. Abhiprerak Gita
5. ASSI SE JAIN GHAT TAK
6. Hopelessness of Arjuna
7. The Soul and It's True Nature
8. Sense of Action (Karma)
9. Action through Wisdom
10. Action through Wisdom
11. THEORY AND PRACTICAL OF EVERY ACTION
12. LOGICAL UNDERSTANDING OF THE SUPREME
13. THE IMPERISHABLE SUPREME
14. Yatra Nishadraj se Hanuman Ghat Tak
15. Yatra Karnatak Ghat se Raja Ghat Tak
16. Yatra Pandey Ghat se Prayagraj Ghat Tak
17. Yatra Ranjendra Prasad Ghat se Dattatreya Ghat Tak
18. YaatraSindhiya Ghat se Gwaliar Ghat Tak
19. Yatra Mangala Gauri Ghat se Hanuman Gadhi Ghat Tak
20. Yatra Gaay Ghat Se Nishad Ghat Tak
21. MAA GANGA, GHATEN EVM UTSAV
22. Ganga Arti Dev Deepavali evam Any Utsav
23. Potentials of Digitalized India
24. VEDIC CONSCIOUSNESS
25. A Brief Introduction to Vedic Science
26. Kashi ke Barah Jyotirling
27. IMPACT OF MOTIVATION
28. Let's have a Milky Way Journey
29. Color Therapy in a Nutshell

ppp

Contact

DR. JAGADEESH PILLAI

MBA & PhD in Vedic Science

Four Times Guinness World Record Holder

Winner of Mahatma Gandhi Vishwa Shanti Puraskar and
Global Peace Ambassador

Gemology, Astro & Vastu Consultant - Spiritual Counselor

Consultant for designing World Record Ideas

Efficient Tarot Card Reader

9839093003

myrichindia@gmail.com

drjagadeeshpillai@facebook

drjagadeeshpillai@instagram
jagadeeshpillai@youtube

www. JAGADEESHPILLAI.com

ᐅᐅᐅ

|| LOKAHA SAMASTHAHA SUKHINO BHAVANTU ||

ॐॐॐ